Dec 2020

Dear Josh & S.J.

Thought you might
appreciate Holly's
Treasured words on
nature —

Blessing to you
in 2021,
Love,
Pat

FAMILIARS

Holly Wren Spaulding

Alice Greene & Co.   Ann Arbor, Michigan

Alice Greene & Co.
P. O. Box 7406
Ann Arbor, MI 48107
www.alicegreene.com

ISBN 978-1-935770-22-0

Cover image © Tate
"Undergrowth," 1941, Eliot Hodgkin (1905-1987)
Presented by the Trustees of the Chantrey Bequest 1943

Editor: Jill Peek
Book Design: Jean Buescher Bartlett
Invisible Angel: Colin O'Brien

Printed in the United States of America

Listen to me. I am telling you
a true thing. This is the only kingdom.
The kingdom of touching;
the touches of the disappearing, things.

—*Aracelis Girmay, "Elegy"*

Contents

Admissions

Testimonials

Foretellings

Admissions

. . . .

*In which a traveler arrives
at the edge of a wildland,
seeking guidance
from its inhabitants
and neighbors.*

Beech

The path ahead
is a ribbon of earth
lit by afternoon sun.

Branches drape down.

A traveler reaches out,
bare wrist, leather glove,
to stroke the oncoming green

as if softly in love.

L a r k

I want to speak
with the plants
and animals

as St. Francis
stroked the hare,
the sow, the robin

who knew somehow
that he was
Friend.

Vine

To touch

the upper
branches

of the tree's

Yes.

A c o r n

Lie down
in leaf litter

dark soil
and bones

begin.

Heather

Not a low fog above all.

The birth of mauve.

Hazel

The one more shimmering
than the other

depending on the light.

Sycamore

Two hundred summers

so children will know
reasons for leaves.

A s h

Defeat comes like rain
over a mountain.

A beetle the size of a thorn.

A d d e r

For protection, inscribe

your hundred names for fear

on a poultice of leaves;

cast into fire.

Bramble

When the fruit
of this body

breaks

from petals
from thickets

comes true

in red, in black,
in layers

of rain
of sun
or night.

Blackberry

Reach into the hedge—

the quick cut,
precise taste in your mouth
will remind you
of a roadside patch
thirty years ago.

Walnut

Why do you come here,
from a thousand miles
to touch this place?

Why should this haven
take you?

Testimonials

· · · · · · · · · · · · · · · · · · · ·

*In which the inhabitants
speak; the traveler listens.*

Holly

On this day
the air smelled
of cut pine.

Every ilex blazed.

The forest spoke
me to me.

I survived
their unbelief.

The longest winter.

Crocus

I traveled cold
dominions
to arrive.

When a woman
leans close
we recognize
each other.

Fern

My tight green
thaws through
layered dark.

Blade then stipe
my fuse unfurls.

The air becomes me.

D o e

I clear small patches
with my mouth.

What else is there
but this field,

this winter,
hunger?

Carnation

I hear your appeals.
A man's name, a child's.
Numbers and deadlines.

And every now and then
an intake of breath,
an audible *mmmmm*.

Take this and continue.

Gorse

Rough and ugly
and rampant all
over the heath

and then we flower,
yellow
and shameless.

P o p p y

In the searchlight
high beams

hot pavement
rim of weeds

the red red red red
of a whole field

alive.

Thrush

Sing, they used to say.

What is dawn without your voice?
What is June?

Until they forgot.

These geese keep landing
in the overgrown field
bodies the same slate gray
as the crates of shingles
left by a neighbor
who died suddenly at forty.

These animals, their language
in the high grass, calling.

This place between
that's not their home
where no one settles
since the widow sold the horses.

This first heat of summer
making blue in the iris,
peonies eaten open by ants.

This three-year-old
who crouches now
to admire new mushrooms
whose smooth tan caps
and hidden gills
she names *Beautiful*.

Clover, alfalfa, rye.
I recognize each resident
of these rough-worked acres.

And rose and snake,
gibbous moon
and wind and stones.
Cricket hum and summer.

The old man who keeps me here
and the woman at the far fence
who waits while her dog

tears at the earth
searching, searching.

I have been to the border,
high heat excruciating,
the light a blade
that cut us all day long.

I asked my questions
and recorded what I saw.

Amidst the thousand dialects
and dying languages
a thrum that needs
no translation.

It has come to this
far shore,
forgotten island.

The atmosphere composed
of something other
than real air.

I smell no estuary.
There are no mangroves here.

Bulbs bathe the world
in too much light.

I search with my black
eyes and amazing bill.

Where are the fish?

Foretellings

. . . .

*In which some questions
are answered; the future
revealed.*

Conker

But in the deeper forest
another way
appears.

O x

Don't think
I never wonder
what else I
might have been.

Catkin

Rain and rain and rain
and inflorescence.
A sense of abandon
all over the ground.

Dandelion

You could work all year
with poison and blades.

Night then late night
and still this yellow
dusted glow,
stems silking
to pink.

Everyone knows
our true name
endures.

They want us gone
but we won't go.

Brook

What else
will hold
it all
in place

when no one
can find
a trickle

to show
a child
how water
moves

shapely and
indispensable

still fluent
in cowslip

and visited
by heron.

Heron

Among
snow-
melt

and stone

my catch
streaks
silver

my river
body

gray-
blue.

Coyotes crying all night
in a landscape of rocks
and scrub oaks.

Dust.

Come here, they said.

Sagebrush
or did she dream it?

Opened both doors,
all the windows,

let wind in.

A slick brown snake
uncoiled on the threshold.

Birds flying fast
from the soffits.

Ancient light,
mountains,
an orange couch.

A warmth she walked into.

A certain kind of person will
survive the Great Derangement,
track me through heat and insects,
mud and underbrush.
They won't care if I'm rough skinned.
A gamey flavor is nothing to them.
A winter's worth of meat, though.

What they don't know is my gift
of premonition. I can tell you
there will be difficult years. Horrors
beyond any already fathomed.
But some time after, blue will flow back,
rare seeds after long dormancy,
pastures laced with sorghum.

You can't imagine what you'll hear
when all the machines stop.
And bees kissing after everything.
Remember the lilacs of childhood?
Like that, but on and on.

C h e e t a h

There are times
that require
you speak the words

and speak them
and speak them.

You have always known
these languages.

They are your
mothertongues.

You are not alone
flinging your bodies
into dark water, murk.

Bats wing overhead,
the shore vibrates with song.

You don't know my kind
or this pool you've crashed
though you shiver at the thought
of what you cannot see

and you are glad for this place
before all that is portended
comes to pass.

This floating in the cool layers,
last light, until you can't.

Beech

Being begins in desire.

A child who died
in winter
returned in May.

It wanted to exist
so built a body.

Rain came
and sun.

Calm comes over
those who pause
beneath its canopy.

Pansy

Ten thousand emissaries,

blue, white, yellow, maroon—

an end to hostilities.

Author's Note

In 2016, I was invited to create an exhibit as part of an artist
residency in northern Michigan. I am not a visual artist, but
for some time I had imagined placing poems in a gallery so that
visitors could walk among them, as they might move through
a sculpture garden or arboretum. The titles of each piece
were words from a list of nature terms that had been recently
displaced from the *Oxford Junior Dictionary* (words like 'crocus'
and 'conker' for example making way for words like 'chatroom');
language seeming to symbolize and further the growing
separation of humanity from the rest of nature. A few poems
from that initial series appear in this book, such as "Acorn,"
"Adder," "Heather," and "Ox."

Holly Wren Spaulding, August 17, 2020

Acknowledgments

I am grateful to the editors and journals where some of these poems first appeared: *Poetry Northwest, Blue Mountain Commons, Mass Poetry, Solitary Plover, Two If By Sea, Carve Magazine* and *Talking River*. "Doe" was published in the book *Imagination & Place: Weather*, edited by Kelly Barth (Imagination & Place Press, 2012). "Sycamore" closed my essay, "The Language of Trees," in *ELEMENTAL: New Creative Nonfiction from Michigan* (Wayne State University Press, 2018).

"Pasture" is for Ever Mirren Lusignan Rigney. "Brook" is dedicated to Juniper Laine Spaulding. "Cheetah" references Margaret Atwood's poem "Marsh Languages." The epigraph comes from Aracelis Girmay's poem, "Elegy," in *Kingdom Animalia* (Boa Editions, LTD., 2011).

I am grateful to the Ann Hall Artist in Residence program, for providing the occasion for me to conceive the first phase of this project and to Melanie Parke and Richard Kooyman for nominating me for that residency. Thank you to my collaborator, William Muller, of Big Wheel Press, who helped me create a letterpress portfolio of *Lost Lexicon* poems in Spring 2017. Thank you to Betsy Ross, The Old Art Building, and The Leelanau Cultural Center in Leland, Michigan, for hosting an exhibition of that work. This book would not exist otherwise. Brit Washburn provided essential moral and editorial support throughout the development of this collection, for which I am most grateful. Thank you to Jim Boorstein, Chris Dombrowski, Amber Edmondson, Joseph Massey, Sharon Oriel, Katey Schultz, Kate Strathmann, Naoe Suzuki, Alison Swan, Brad Watson, and Peter Wyer for vital conversations along the way. Blue Mountain Center, Pentaculum, Nancy Lustgarten and Ned DeLaCour offered shelter while I worked on this project. Thank you to Jill Peek, Colin O'Brien, and Alice Greene & Co. for believing in this book from the beginning. My parents, Carol and Joseph Spaulding, planted the seeds for every sentiment in this book, long ago. My deepest appreciation goes to my beloved, Matt Rigney, for getting it and getting me and joining me in this life.

About the Author

HOLLY WREN SPAULDING is a writer, interdisciplinary artist,
and founder of Poetry Forge, where she offers virtual writing
workshops and a manuscript incubator. Her publications include
If August (Alice Greene & Co., 2017) and several chapbooks.
Her writing has appeared in *The New York Times*, *Michigan
Quarterly Review*, *Witness*, *The Ecologist*, *New Internationalist*,
and in the books, *We Are Everywhere: The Irresistible Rise of
Global Anti-capitalism* (Verso, 2003) and *ELEMENTAL: New
Creative Nonfiction from Michigan* (Wayne State University
Press, 2018). Hailing from the Leelanau Peninsula of Michigan,
she now lives in southern Maine with her family.